Alice in Ruby Slippers

Alice in Ruby Slippers

Poems by

Carol Lynn Stevenson Grellas

Cover design by Shay Culligan
Cover art "The Red Shoes" by Francesco Longo Mancini

ISBN: 978-1-950462-77-3

KELSAY BOOKS
502 South 1040 East, A-119
American Fork, Utah, 84003

Kelsaybooks.com

for my mother

⤳⤶

"Why sometimes I've believed as many as six
impossible things before breakfast."
—Lewis Carroll, *Alice in Wonderland*

"A heart is not judged by how much you love;
but by how much you are loved by others."
—L.Frank Baum, *The Wizard of Oz*

Acknowledgments

Better than Starbucks: "My Mother's Scolding Spoon," "Don't Call the Doctor"

Angle: "Sonnet of Unrest"

Touch the Journal of Healing: "The Cancer Diagnosis"

Lucid Rhythm: "Evening Bell"

Eunioa Revew: "Calypso's Flight"

Las Cruces Poets and Writers Magazine: "The Box beneath My Bed"

Weasel Press: "Strange Fruit"

The Orchards Poetry Journal: "Elegy to a Poem without an End," "Farewell to Fear

Raintown Review: "Utopia's Demise"

Angle: "For Kathy"

The Moon Magazine: "Pandemonium"

Lucid Rhythm: "Final Girl"

New Poetry: "Odalisque"

Better than Starbucks: "Too Soon"

Local Gems Press: "Halloween Sonnet"

Chantarelle's Notebook: "Charlatan"

Joyful: "Forever-things"

Poetry Super Highway: "Thanksgiving with Hugo"

Weasel Press: "Dear Sir"

Mezzo Cammin: "On Underestimating the Aftermath," "Plaques and Tangles"

The Scruffy Dog Review: "Lost in Kansas"

Midwest Poetry: "Alice in Ruby Slippers"

Bumbershoots: "Will Work for Ants"

Epistemology of an Odd Girl, Hasty Notes: "Six Impossible Things"

Other Books by Carol Lynn Stevenson Grellas

Epistemology of an Odd Girl, March Street Press

A Thousand Tiny Sorrows, March Street Press

Hasty Notes in No Particular Order, Aldrich Press

Letters Under the Banyan Tree, Aldrich Press

The Wanderer's Dominion, Aldrich Press

On the Edge of the Ethereal, Aldrich Press

Breakfast in Winter, 1st edition Flutter Press, 2nd edition, Woodhaven Press

Litany of Finger Prayers, Pudding House Press

Object of Desire, Finishing Line Press

Epitaph for the Beloved, Finishing Line Press

The Nightly Suicides, Kattywompus Press

Things I Can't Remember to Forget, Prolific Press

Before I Go to Sleep, the winning chapbook in The Red Ochre Chapbook Contest

An Ode to Hope in the Midst of Pandemonium, Main Street Rag

In the Making of Goodbyes, Clare Songbirds Publishing House

The Butterfly Room, Big Table Publishing

Contents

Part One

Part Two

∽∾

Part One

Lost in Kansas

Dearest Glinda, good witch of the North,
I dream of you forever-young,

bright red-haired queen of noble worth
with bluest eyes, and gowned in white

beyond the bluebird's rainbow flight.
Come wave your wand through talking

trees and flying monkeys in the night.
I'm lost within these wicked winds—

tornado-life no radar-dome,
I've clicked my heels not once but thrice,

and still can't find a place called home,
and still can't find a place called home.

My Mother's Scolding Spoon

She used to chase me with a wooden spoon,
a game of cat and mouse, until the time
I watched the handle break one afternoon.
It made me laugh, though laughing was a crime
when I was young if making fun of her
implied a gain. A penalty I'd come
to know could be reversed. A saboteur,
I learned to watch for indications from
the way she'd say my name. Her lips would purse
unyielding, then I'd know, I'm done,
no glimmer of hilarity. She'd curse
surprisingly, "Goddammit!" if I'd won
or broke the spell. I've saved her favorite things,
her watch, and spoon, and all that memory brings.

Sonnet of Unrest

I guesstimate the distance from the frond
to roots entrenched and tangled deep beneath
the tombstone where my mother sleeps. Beyond
the counterpane of greenery, a wreath
beside her grave adorns an easel made
of wood that venerates another life.
Misunderstood, today I choose to wade
among the dead instead of facing strife
at home, the struggle of who's wrong or right;
small differences that escalate from loud
to louder still until eclipsed by night—
yet, there's comfort stepping through a crowd
reclined, where no one speaks though right beside,
hereafter leaving differences aside.

Otherworldly

for Sister

A sacred mother, I was drawn to her
beliefs and understood a boundless love
whenever she was close. She called me near
then moved across the room in veils. Above
her waist, a dangling crucifix reflected light
in waves each time she breathed. She said my name
and whispered, *this will help you pray at night*—
gifting me a rosary the same
as hers. She placed it in my tiny palm
and kissed my face, the way a butterfly
might land, then leave again. I felt her calm
abiding grace; grace, a lullaby
she chanted, *God is Good, God is Great*.
My father had just died; I was eight.

Since You've been Gone

Since you died, I've dreamt of being lost—
amid the unfamiliar; somewhere Frost
might call a traveler's puzzlement, a quest
determining which pathway suits me best
as though I've heard an inner voice or song
yet overwhelmed which choice is right or wrong—
bewildered by the thought, I'll cry for you
as if your death's a thing I could undo.
A dream can be a devastating place
though more alarming still to wake and face
the truth of what is real. There's no way
to signal you for help. Sometimes I play
old messages to hear your voice again—
as if you're home, then ask you where you've been.

James Joyce and Nora Have a Heart-to-Heart in Heaven

"An erotic letter by author James Joyce sent to his wife
has fetched a record £240,800 at auction in London."
—*The Irish Times,* Friday, July 9, 2004

You said I was your muse, your dirty girl,
a little whore, a blackguard, chambermaid
seducing you where endless love unfurled,
all good behaviors tossed aside, unobeyed
revealed in letters sold at Sotheby's
where auctioneers cheered ogling over words
emblazoned meant to woo me past our *Bloomsday*
tryst. Epistolary notes that stirred
untold naughty thoughts. Obscenities must
elicit true salaciousness in those
exposed to crudeness from the upper crust.
Yet, dare I say your finest prose
was birthed by pure desire for my kisses—
without my love, there'd never be *Ulysses.*

Twenty Months of Stillness

I kneel before her pink Camilla tree
then grip the leaves she once held in her hand,

where petals thrive in morning's soft decree.
I try another time to understand

the nature of all beauty in a life
that culminates by severance in the end—

with queries, if all blessings born from strife
will supplement our courage to transcend.

Infirmity transforms with final peace
through quelling chronic pain as death its song.

Now once the tree that only bloomed in spring
is filled with mother's flowers all year long.

Repercussions

He dubbed it cancer when the door was closed—
in murmured voice with echo's haunting curse.
A power undiminished though opposed
in quiet as we heard that word traverse,
negotiate around the room and back
against the walls it ricocheted, it was,
lived, breathed; a megalomaniac
unleashed, revealed, we heard—and yet because
the repetition lastly ceased, of sound
of cells, of images in waves from then
to now, I cannot help but think we found
a way to real gratitude again—
to love each other louder than before,
and in the midst of silence even more.

The Warrior Gene

What does it mean to have genetic code
predisposing man to murder man?
Could it be true that bloodlines are bestowed
with evil cells blooming in the womb,
or are corrupt surroundings more to blame?
Might some congratulate the mammas still
with babies carrying tainted chromosomes
creating *good old boys* who yearn to kill?
Will science someday say, annihilate
the ones who carry death inside their hearts
determined by a test, or is that hate?
Would outcomes change by just a healthy start?
If Hitler's mother loved him more,
would there have been a second World War?

The Cancer Diagnosis

We linger in the waiting room before
results are in, and there I take your hand
in mine unsure of fate or what's in store—
the two of us with braided arms that land
as one upon my lap. You turn the ring
around my finger as it spins soft glints
of gold reflecting back and forth, a ping
returning light from yours to mine in stints
of milliseconds, yet there's no reply
as you and I communicate without
the need for words. With just a sigh,
I feel a weighty breath of doubt—
uneasiness beyond each pending quest
when nothing said conveys all thoughts repressed.

Don't Call the Doctor, Don't Call the Nurse

It's troublesome to watch my mother age,
and there are days I have to bite my tongue
preventing truths from breaking through, a sage
performance having faltered once among
delivering bad news, removing hope
as if the moral thing to do is mute
all words of reasoning to better cope
with something looming overhead. Elope
instead from any notion of disease.
Incurable sounds better left unsaid.
Discount the need for any expertise,
avoid all talk of what may lie ahead!
And so, we go about our day this way,
evading every medical dismay.

Evening Bell, Riding Home

I'm dying here without you by my side,
bedewed with tears, a masquerade each day.
I read psalm twenty-three, and then you died,
with desperateness I've come to you to say,

ride back to me. I'm knocking at His door—
your carriage must be near. I've heard the sound
of galloping approaching once before,
the sacred journey soaring Heaven-bound.

I'll wait beside your marker carved in stone,
an epitaph adorns the home you claim,
all darkness creeps the more I am alone—
I've seen a granite tombstone with my name.

Lone angel, I am pleading with you now,
please send an evening vesper whereupon
you'll tie a rope of stars from every bough,
and have your horseman pull the one I'm on.

Calypso's Flight

If you'd have called my name, I might have known
before you saw a breadth of sky, then flown
above the neighbor's house. A gust below
your wings, I might have lassoed feathers slow
between my hands. Because an impulse took
you there, I've never had the chance to look
at you and say, come back old bird. Dear god!
I prayed inside my head. What sweet façade
replaced your perch, a slant of tile sable?
Hapless being, while flaunting on the gable,
then waning far from view. You'd carried through
I'd thought, some reverie adorned in blue—
but you had burned, outstretched atop their roof.
They brought you home in case I needed proof.

The Box beneath My Bed

Inside a box beneath my bed
possessions hide that once were hers—
although I know that she lies dead,
I lift the lid and memory blurs.

An evening bag, a string of pearls
a veil she wore the day she wed,
now souvenirs, this lonely girl's
unspoken thoughts were never said.

Sometimes the box beneath my bed
will summon me, I've heard the call;
it taps the frame below my head
a sacred place, my wailing wall.

We speak in whispers, secret prayers.
Clandestine meetings in my room
are taking place on empty chairs—
she leaves the scent of her perfume.

I'm Breathing In and Out Alone

Just like the bud in early days of spring
whose head must yearn for rays of dawning light,
I've come from darkness wanting everything
for knowing life drifts sadly in the night
then finds its way with beacons from a star
directing towards a love that pulls us near,
like angels moving closer from afar
with lilies on their feet; they show no fear
while strolling to a place behind the Sun—
he touches them with fingers made of gold.
I've seen an aura walking with no one,
a secret that I've kept and never told—
and like the flower growing on the vine
someday I know I'll hold their hand in mine.

Strange Fruit

for Billie Holiday

Because a ballad uncovered her pain
        exposing racism, evil and sin,

because she crooned without fancy refrain
        a song of murder while dying within,

they squirmed in their chairs while nobody dared
        acknowledge the truth, confronting the wrong,

she stood in the dark and sang them a prayer
        then one by one, they applauded her song.

Elegy to the Poem Without an End

after reading *The Second Coming,* by William Butler Yeats

But if you'd seen the falcons' eyes, the way
their pupils pinned and tapered, killers loose;
gyres spinning, while unstoppable their path,
unchangeable as brutes in search of prey,
and absolute since all succumb to death
no matter if a Bethlehem awaits.
Infinity is just a figure 8,
cold fingers traced against my breath.
How pondering eternity's more harrowing
than promising a reason to believe,
although there is no proof beyond the grave,
disaster ever looms its narrowing
prognosticates the ending of a turn—
denying what's in motion will return.

The Promise

If I am only part of everything
and nothing more, well darling, what of that?
When I have you, the two of us, this ring
the sum that signifies the whole whereat
we're joined as one forever though we sing
our separate song. An aria, I've heard,
becomes an opus, melodies we bring,
a gift together with the other's word—
your promise made that joins us till we die.
Although beyond this life, a paradise
I hope will reunite us once again
since you are all I have. The compromise
is this; there's always one who's left behind
with only memories as they rewind.

Watermark

Oh, love, I write of my imperfect prayer
that I may lie beside you every hour—
as breezes bait the bending of a bloom
and lift the petals of each breathless flower.

Because a butterfly arrives to tease,
yet granted moments in suspended flight
while hovering, it lands upon my skin,
celestial fluttering, so impolite—

as gentle as the berry's fleshy-seed,
my heart upon the bough awaits your hand—
though wary of all passing promises
portending diadems bejeweled withstand

the tempest's onset underneath the sky—
where cobalt paints a canvas for the moon.
Allow me this one hope my Oberon,
decree forever born this afternoon.

Dare I let such whimsy tease my soul,
a damsel fraught with dreams of ecstasy
while chariots arrive through billowed clouds
and you, my love, become the reverie.

Of You, Just Because

She used to push a light around my heart
igniting words that later found a place
and made their way beyond a secret part
of me that lived within a hidden space,
as if she'd freed me from the looming dark,
and yet I doubt she ever knew the weight
she'd lifted. Name it love, her spark
of magic passing through to me, a fate
I'm grateful for each day. I'd like to write
a verse, intricate, yet understood—
a dedication beautiful as night
with gentle love so infinite and good.
Sometimes a life is graced with such a friend—
with faith, she'll know me from this poem penned.

Utopia's Demise

Oh, Pamela, I've not forgotten how
we dressed our dolls, the bonnets knitted, each
one tied with ribbons fixed, the plastic brow
that framed their sleepy lids, the way we'd preach

to them pretending they'd done wicked things,
your room a home of stars and storybooks,
red licorice from Thrifty's, pocket rings
you'd hung from sconces lit, your crochet hook

for sewing blankets in your trundle drawers
with feathered down, old roller-skates long worn
beneath a closetful of pinafores,
your hair pinned up with tendrils barely clipped

behind your ears, and how we'd brush each other's
ringlets till our curls held the sunlight's reign,
the eager way we waited for our mother's
yes, consent to board the weekend train,

and how we'd one day vanish, no goodbyes—
we might have known to never close our eyes.

For Kathy

There was a girl who loved me once,
from piano keys and fiddleback
chairs with gardenias pinned on strands
of hair, who chanted songs in longneck
pearls she knotted twice in kimono robes
and gorgeous curls, so naughty-nice
she lit up rooms and drank her drink
on afternoons in china cups of rosehip
tea with a dose of honey or maybe three.
There was a girl who loved me then,
with initials tattooed on her skin. She
sang undressed, beneath the moon—
I miss that girl who died too soon.

Farewell to Fear

If I should wake from slumber's death alone
to find no other occupant or throne
imagined where a Jesus ought to be,
replaced by nothingness, not you or me
entwined in afterlife with memories
of body, mind or soul, faith's guarantee
defunct, in fact, a useless exercise
believing in a plethora of lies—
well then, the sorry risk in wanting more
is overlooking all that's come before—
indifferent to a dazzling kind of day
where expectations amplify dismay.
If earth is only this, I must amend.
Love is all that matters in the end.

Pandemonium

There'll be a day my boy becomes a man,
imposing wonderment inside a narrow line—
beyond the road that disappears ahead,
one path where truth and reverie entwine—
more challenging than mothers dare to say
as disappointment looms in evening's sky
where once a wish was made upon a star,
if only it were easier…and I
am just a girl beneath this woman's form
where miracles have flourished in my womb,
so unaware the world would be unfair,
a topsy-turvy realm chock-full of doom—
yet hope can be the visionary's flare.
So, dream, I tell my boy, of all you dare.

What-if Tales

The countless hours spent, a worry-fest;
unsolved dilemmas pondered as each woe
ensues. All anguish robbing any rest
or peaceful moment where the heart may know
serenity. For provocation finds
some solace if the soul's allowed to dance
where dreams might flourish when the mind's
at rest or amplified—imaginings enhance
the hopefulness that spectacles might reign
past fear, per sleeps request when nightmares pale.
Tranquility still shares Illusion's name
beyond our consciousness or waking jail.
For heaven bodes its restfulness through bliss—
where endless troubles die. Remember this.

Letter to a Tree

Dear tree, because I happened by one day
and noticed how your glory filled the sky—
the way the wind had begged your boughs to sway
in softest rhythms of a lullaby,

imagining that I was hanging from
a twig transformed from body to a leaf—
well how magnificent to then succumb
transformed to beauty born of your motif

suspended by a sprawling amber wing,
a sail exposed unto the gusty sea
unsteady with each breath beyond the spring—
yet, how majestic you appeared to me.

Today, I happened by you once again
observing you'd undressed the scenery,
imposing still by claiming your terrain
with leaves, a coverlet of greenery.

Final Girl

I dream I am the heroine, the one
whose scream lives past the end, defying odds
and cut off heads, the needle pit, a prom undone—
forget the deaths along the way, the Gods
are helpless through this reel, don't waste a prayer
for superstars who never seem to lose
their breath despite the slasher's rants that scare
the cast who dare to right the wrong or choose
a hapless route condemned. Each scene unfurls
to horrors played, where killers never leave
an out for teenage boys, but final girls
are always spared. The females take reprieve—
beyond *The Ring, What Lies Beneath* is grim,
but rest assured that final girl will win.

Rapunzel

Because her mother longed for Rampion
Because her garden walled a life within

Because her birth was traded for a soul
Because her father's sin was that he stole

Because her beauty soon became a curse
Because her years were tainted for the worse

Because her hair unfastened brushed the ground
Because her braid could wind past windows down

Because her voice would hoist an angel's wings
Because her singing lured the sons of Kings

Because her melodies were magical instead
Because her prince would sneak in skeins of thread

Because her heart was trapped inside a wall
Because her promise given caused a fall

Because her splendor only gave her pain
Because her plan unfolded with her mane

Because her tresses begged a scissor's snip
Because her tongue was boastful with a slip

Because her captor prized another's ache
Because her lover planned their great escape

Because her plaits were knotted like a rope
Because her exile left him without hope

Because her weeping filled the woodland air
Because her spirit found him waiting there

Because her love unearthed what came before
Because her tower never had a door.

Ode to the Flower

Chrysanthemum with petals sweetly clustered
how you dance on windy days, like children
welcoming the breeze of spring, yet flustered

when a waft of air undoes the aura
though you bend with all the grace of summer
nearing fall in awe, oh fragrant flora.

Mimosa, you're a tree so ever shy
with leaves too sensitive; we ought naught touch,
naivety a virtue. Virgin beauties to the passerby.

I shall admire every pinkish sphere
allowing distance for your timid blush
but still, I find your fearful ways most dear

coquettish as a girlish- bloom for all to fawn,
perhaps you peek through secret clouds at dawn.
Bright daffodil with upturned trumpet bell

where angels harken for your sunlit notes—
a trail of bees make love to you, the swell
of yellowness that bleeds from petal tips.

How glorious to hold you in my hand
behold the softness of each bloom that slips
along my fingers. How I'd love to wear

your sunlit shade all woven deep with ribbons,
ornaments of you through washed and braided hair,
a golden chord that beckons Heaven's grass

for one who grows within the blades of green
carefree as though a life will never pass.
If I could live like you instead of me

so gratified with just the love from every bee.
The lily, purist thing I've ever seen
a fleur-de-lis extraordinaire so pale

your reign as regal as a country's queen,
even so, your helplessness prevails sometimes
because you are among the blessed group

with cemeteries calling you. God chimes
his church-bells from Cathedrals in the sky
to those who find you comforting. You go

when death has made a home for you to lie
above their dwelling as they rest alone.
You keep them company dressed up in white,

perfume the air with ecstasy-cologne.
The birds create an aria around
your sacred place where children come and wait—

and now I'll lie my tired body down
that I may hear the sleeping of the dead
beneath your bloom, upon each grassy bed.

The Sequoia

While sunlight crept atop her tousled hair
she dreamt of grassy woodlands, to be free,

where life appeared more simple breathing air
from branches of the grandest living tree.

Then sliding naked toes beneath the earth,
her legs became magnificently strong,

transporting her to Heaven like a birth
while branches beckoned birds to sing their song.

Because she never held the light that way
through bars of golden beams across the sod,

she disappeared forever on the day
communion with a tree brought her to God.

Part Two

Odalisque

What hour is this that brings a jaundiced glow?
The sun has found us through the maidenhair,
disturbing all the camouflage of night
to notify our rousing. Lady Faire,
your window raps, intruders with perfume
awakening each flower through the glass,
where last a moon rock's shadow graced your hair
obsidian's dark blackish veil will pass.

And I must find a purpose to go on
another day to mourn, your devotee.
As if the evening's gift of this soiree—
one last remembrance left will set me free.
My love, I fear a death unless you're near
unworthy as I am, you must comply.
Without you, I'll surrender to the day—
estranged and left alone to surely die.

Oh listen, hear the harpsichord, it plays;
our opus is a symphony for two,
and though I am a shameful fool, succumb
before a moment blinks the morning through
or solitude will push throughout my veins.
A spirit without verve won't feel at all,
so blinded by the loneliness, I'll chide
the atmosphere that yields its murky pall

since nothing of my life will ever grow
beyond this longing tarnishing my soul.
If blooming till the bursting is replete,
a probing bee, your drone, my queen, this role—
will only prove my valor by your side
when close you lie beside me as obsessed
am I, forgive me, for my cowardice,
yet you are like a goddess when undressed.

Too Soon

I read his note that said, *my brother's death*
is imminent, advising every friend
and distant kin before his final breath.
I'm sorry for your loss, I typed, hit send
without a way make to amends. The hand
is quicker than the eye, and second thoughts
prove axioms don't lie. An ampersand
should follow with some blue forget-me-nots
or prayers of sorrow offered, but instead…
such an idiotic thing to say—
and nothing's more pathetic or cliché
even when appropriately said.
So, I tried again then hit reply…
Forgive me for my premature goodbye!

You Are Almost Gone to Her

In ignorance, she viewed you as her friend,
yet, rarely moments indicated love,
though there were days affection felt a blend
implying you were capable thereof.
She often wondered how you spent your time—
divided by what's left après your need?
For fawning triumph must be so sublime
from one whose only fan is guaranteed.
And years become much weightier with age
when boys turn into men who might replace
their youthfulness with providence and sage,
the holy grail for lives they've led, embraced.
Yet you have never acted as a brother,
though bloodlines named you siblings by a mother.

As If the Hours Wait

after reading, *Because I could not stop for death*
—Emily Dickinson

As if the hours wait unmoved
the days have blurred to one,
the driver never offered me
a chance to turn around—

perhaps I would have begged for time
before the carriage came,
unwound the ever-moving clock
that chimes a mortal's name.

I would have said farewell to fields
beneath the yellowed sun—
I would have harbored jealousy
the Deities would shun.

What citizen is seized so quick
devoid the common pleas?
One would hope for Paradise
to call within the breeze.

No penalty would seem unfair,
denying His request.
Surrendering death's interview—
baptized eternal guest.

Joy Ride

If I could drive the hearse, I would,
I'd wear a scarf of red,
and shout through windows rolled for air,
"this passenger's not dead!"

Oh, the speeding wheels would fly
across the winding course
and I would steer the hearse along
as if it were a horse.

We'd jump the clouds and weave about
the Heavens for our breath,
and I would tell you tales along
your journey marked as death.

And none would know my darling dear,
what happened on that day
for they will find a vacant car
and wonder what to say.

But you and I will be long gone—
behind a trail of leaves
just parted where the tires made
a lambent path for thieves.

I'll be accused of burglary
by shoals of mourners when
we take our flight beyond the eaves
of every home we've been.

If asked to drive the hearse I will,
unless I'm in the casket
well then, my darling, you must be
the one who is the escort.

Halloween Sonnet

In evenings mist beyond the starry skies,
I sometimes catch a glimmering of eyes
that one might say is just a twinkling space
behind a ghostly cloud and yet a face
approximating just a hint of you
appears behind the silhouette of blue.
Because I've called your name in moonlight's creep
imagining your rising from death's sleep
as if you'd found a way to leave your tomb
and exit midnight's portal to my room
I wonder if I might make one request—
an apparition makes a charming guest
especially on a lonesome Halloween,
please visit me if only in my dream.

Charlatan

I'd like to tell you off, without a doubt,
and yet I'm slightly hopeful there's a chance
you'll change. I might regret your finding out
all names assigned behind your back. One glance
my way would surely indicate distaste
for you if countenance the weatherglass
of trust. Relationships can be a waste
when dealing with a self-important ass
who never bothers noticing there's life
outside the narcissistic reach of one
conceited counterpart. Another's strife
of no concern whose heart is ever numb
to matters he rebuffs as justly small—
in fact, a real jerk, above it all.

Up in the Air

Perhaps it's just the way a raindrop holds
a glint of light when moonlight skims its lamp
that makes you feel a tiny tear escaped
from Heaven, turning breezy grasses damp—
to any living being who wonders why
these things are never easily explained
occurring in small fragments of a day
as if the mysteries of life ordained

illuminate what possibly might be
coincidence, a twist of fate, a dose
colliding just precisely when you'd think
it strange another episode so close
occurred in sync with burdens on your mind—
intrusions all, but timed exactly when
you're worried for another's destiny
as doom might intervene that second. Then

because you see an envelope of red
take flight and topple in a bird-like fall
inside a store, the card's marked *sympathy*—
assuming now you might receive a call
concerning what will only be grim news—
the way that envelope turned dark, that hue
of blood, and there's a message left at home,
a prophecy? Since you already knew.

Forever-things

I'll cast my soul upon an unmoored stone
as if the bruising never meant to be
will mend with trust and guidance from His throne
becalmed by love and synchronicity,

till then I'll count the days when angels come
regardless of this wingless realm on Earth;
imprisoned, then awakened, gorgeous dove—
forever-things bring frankincense and mirth.

Because this ceaseless song is ever-heard,
how wicked is the ear that turns away
the flutist's tune that haunts all chapel walls
through vesper-bells when summoning the day.

I'm yearning for the crags to pummel bones,
collapsing unto all that's left of me,
and there I'll heal within the water's grave
as fate and I are one beneath the sea.

Thanksgiving with Hugo

Dear Hugo, grace was always in your heart
enchanting everyone who knew you then—
long years before your life was torn apart—
yet fortitude, a lesson you would lend.
And I was but a child in your path.
God placed me near the hearth inside your home
for fire burnt so brightly from your core
beyond the realm of anyone I'd known.
Where memories revealed from within
were spoken with a whispered voice in tears
remembering the agonies you'd seen
exposing horrors lived through yesteryears—
while I was seated firmly by your side
one dinner on Thanksgiving as you kissed
my hand and spoke of gratitude for man—
I saw the numbers etched above your wrist.

Dear Sir

I was so rushed the day I passed you by
although I stopped and listened to your tune.
Harmonicas produce a lovely sound—
so sweet, the way you held that metal spoon
and snapped a pulsing tempo trouble-free,
my ears were full the way tobacco leaves
might smoke inside a pipe then surge through air
for all who stood within your range to eaves-
drop. Still, your face has lingered in my mind—
I should have stopped and offered you a smile,
since searching for you many afternoons,
uncertain of your whereabouts awhile
though you would not remember me, dear Sir
your essence has remained beyond a blur.

For Larnell Bruce Jr.

"killed in a senseless act of violence, based on the color of his skin."
—Larnell Bruce Junior Foundation

The headlines said *the cause of death was hate,*
a boy whose murder sickens me to read—
whose daddy stays at home alone to wait
unaccepting of the fate that's been decreed
as if his son will be returning soon
while visiting his mother on a trip.
Instead, run over by racist goon
who drove his Wrangler like a battleship.
A devastating article to read,
the killing of a child just nineteen
outside a store where both had disagreed,
a routine ending, hardly unforeseen.
His father's comments made me cry today—
just proud his son had tried to walk away.

Noel

It suddenly occurred to me
my doorway birthed a Christmas Tree.
And though it's lovely every year
whose purpose fills a room with cheer
perhaps it's best to let it grow
and leave the roots intact below
where all the other greenery
boasts natural delivery.
I barely squeezed it through the door
with branches broken on the floor—
laborious the entrance made,
dead upon my floor it laid.
Oh, Christmas Tree, before you fell,
the forest heard you cry, "Noel!"

Bearing That Which Is Unbearable

And now as death declares itself again
while mourners stand above a shallow grave
with dandelions gold as diadems

that punctuate the earth in hallowed waves,
where unawakened bodies each to each
lie helpless past the living they forgave,

there is no calming prayer in comforts' reach
if supplication's meant to quell the air.
For grief becomes impossible to breach

when sky is filled with catastrophic prayer.
Despondency soon overwhelms my soul,
but what have I to offer while I'm here?

A plethora of memories unfurl
existing in a body made for being
uneven as its garment's threaded burl

where coverings may camouflage unseen
all sufferings unsightly to the heart
as dying, life's ironic offering.

A promised path no matter where the start
will lead us through an unknown odyssey,
our journey home, preamble's counterpart.

No hapless-fate elixir aids a plea
reclaiming stolen breath already quashed
prognosticating all we cannot see—

this daily dance above the buried mossed.
Within, without, forever yet unnamed,
aghast by loving's sacrificial cost,

where something lost is never something gained.
I place a rose atop her wooden box
preparing for the holiness ordained

by godly men devoid of sinful thoughts,
while mindful how imperfect I must seem
when picking up a smattering of rocks,

then drop them on her casket as I scream.

Little Bird Who Flew beyond My Reach

Because I wrote a poem for you today,
it filled my head with memories of when
you found an opening to disobey
and lost yourself to freedom from within.

When just a chance to pilot your saved heart
became a calling louder than my own
as if you heard a harbinger impart
a hallowed humming from a gilded throne.

And you were so oblivious to sky,
a prisoner kept inside your cage all day
without the opportunity to fly
though often you would flirt with a bouquet

that graced the window's ledge outside my room.
Although I trusted you with doors ajar,
your little body so adorned with plume
it seems you yearned for life beyond a star—

yet how was I to know you waited there
as if we both could find our home in air.

Hope Against Hope

"Hold fast to dreams, for if dreams die
life is a broken-winged bird that cannot fly."
—Langston Hughes

If hope's a thing with feathers,
I'd like to rip its wings,
and make it stay just one more day
to sing and sing and sing...

Although Pandora locked the jar, its lid
screwed tightly shut for reasons of safekeeping
a bit slipped through, an ounce or two, an evil
seen as beautiful, a woman's trick, intriguing.

Yet in the Book of Common Prayer,
since hope's akin to trust,
eternity seems promising
to dust, to dust, to dust.

Dear swallow, I have only this fine coat
to cover me till apple blossoms bloom—
a spendthrift now I'll sell it guessing spring
has entered with your songbird's splendid plume.

Adrift, a sailor lost at sea
in stormy times may grieve
deprived without some anchoring—
believe, believe, believe...

In desperate days I've scrutinized in vain
some promised place kept deep within my breast,
but *spring of hope,* eternal's boundless gift
was missing from its case, a hollowed chest.

They took my mother's hope away
when doctors said no cure—
I whispered to a butterfly,
save her, save her, save her...

And what of all desires pled, undone?
And what of all that goes beyond, unheard?
And what of every wish that rests on faith—
if hope's a thing with feathers, just a bird.

Autopsy

My mother told me not to fib
or I'd go straight to hell,
and never ever twist the truth
from all that was to tell—

and I believed this golden rule
was one I shouldn't break,
because she had no tolerance
for stories that were fake.

I guess I never questioned her
assuming she was right,
that everything she said to me
was honest and forthright.

Now looking back, I've come to find
a day she told a whopper—
one falsehood that I've later learned
was totally improper.

At least if one's accountable
to 'practice what you preach,'
and shouldn't mothers say and do
exactly as they teach?

And I was just a child then
the morning I recall—
I went to wake my father up,
who slept across the hall.

I opened up their bedroom door
then turned the knob just so,
the morning light came spilling through
and cast a shadowed glow.

I tiptoed gently to the bed,
my everyday routine
then leaned in close to kiss his cheek
to stir him from a dream.

But he just slept and never moved—
his hands felt limp and dead,
and when I tried to waken him,
he didn't move his head.

My mother made me leave the room
until the stretcher came.
Away he went with blinking lights,
a siren's flashing flame.

She said he'd had a heart attack,
and offered nothing more
yet when she died, I found his note—
long hidden in her drawer.

With all her fiery threats of hell…
one truth had been denied.
The records read *Took Overdose.*
Apparent Suicide.

A Mother's Message to Her Son

The mother doesn't care about the gender
when it comes to loving her unborn child.
She's not a scientist or any kind of God
just a flowerbed to cherish what may grow
no matter timid, calm or wild, boy, or girl,
what life may come to her by way of prayers.

The world imperfect though, as if her prayers
might help prepare a life no matter gender.
And then, with a gentle grin, *It's a girl,*
the doctor says and rests upon her chest, a child.
She'll teach her all she knows, but what will grow
within a life of labels, past the mysteries of a God?

Her universe creating judgments, not by God
but those who say they know the way of prayers—
hypocrites, uncaring if a life may reassign or grow
into itself, the way each flower's meant to be. Gender
unimportant in a mother's eyes, her child
was part of heaven in her womb, boy, or girl

a gift. A secret kept then shared, the way a girl
might blush when gazing at the darkened sky and seeing God.
No, mothers cannot name which path a child
takes, nor the chance of shooting stars when saying prayers.
Love is never love imposed by rules or roles. Gender
must be nurtured then allowed to grow.

And when a daughter says she's found a way to grow
her happiness, rename herself a boy, that girl
should know her mother stands beside her gender
choice, celebrates all she wants to be in front of God
or anyone. A mother doesn't care but says her prayers
to give her daughter strength, guard her child,

protect her from the world. The spirit of a child,
no matter pronouns, he or she will always grow,
will not be crushed, more glorious than prayers
or lilacs on a hill. Where once confined, a girl
transformed to boy. Now a mother looks to God
and says her love remains unchanged by gender.

She will love him, what's the difference, girl or boy? Gender
mustn't force a hostage-heart but travel free as God to prayers—
She revels in her child's bravery to know,
her son's courageousness to grow.

On Underestimating the Aftermath

I was daughter then nursemaid to parents who died
as a gallant attempt though my efforts relied
on instructions from doctors whose manuals I read
when sent home as a reference yet much left unsaid—

with regard to behaviors that one shouldn't see
if one's hoping to salvage a last memory.
As if being the carer for someone in need
might be noted in heaven, a virtuous deed.

For disease of the brain, an unmalleable force,
I required a booklet, a guide with a course,
or a sundowner's channel explaining the mind
where directions were given or may be defined.

When the light dimmed to shadows, each ominous dawn
with our daily disorder eroding the calm
overwhelming our closeness, invasion of roles
soon the parent's the child, and the child's the mole,

to myself, I'd endeavored most dutiful chores—
being kind and forbearing while forging through tears.
With all tumbledown memories turned tainted from sweet
where most visits made heartened by thoughtful conceit.

But when dying was over, their eulogy read…
there was no one to tell me, good girl. They were dead.

Plaques and Tangles

Her father plays such childish games
among his rounds of forgotten names
and swears there's nothing wrong—a stance
she hopes to overturn, her chance
at saving him, or what remains.

She throws out matches, though he claims
he'll never lose his home to flames.
In-between a vacant glance,
her father plays

with given pills. Despite all claims,
confusion lasts. Still, she blames
ill-fated cerebral circumstance
on genetics' role, not happenstance.
Dementia's hymn, a dazed refrain
her father plays.

Without Vision

Sometimes beneath the sheltering of skin,

      a secret illness writes itself in Braille

soundless as the unseen breath of trees,

it lives, grows, sighs and breathes within

      the shadow of the body's fleshy veil

imprisoning a mortal enemy—

overlooked, a bleed below the quick

      where unjust rooted suffering prevails—

in a hidden disability

      inaudible, with desperate need to speak.

      Help Me.

The Minutes Saved

Once, she missed the sound of hours
the way her hands could tap to time,
once she longed for noisy towers
that sang with bells of godly chime.

Here she thought her soul could keep
the tick and tock of long lost days,
here she thought her mind could reap
the moments' used forgotten ways,

and so she stole his kitchen clock
that had its place above the door,
a tiny space that housed a cock
who danced around a little floor.

She swallowed all the inner parts,
gold hooks with weights, and measured rings.
Now every time the movement starts
inside her heart, the cuckoo sings.

Alice in Ruby Slippers

Oh, girl who sips her beautiful soup,
and walks a winding yellow-brick road—
who dreams of tweedles that loop-de-loop,
where munchkins sing in turtle code.

The griffin calls to Neverland
she's now confused, could this be Oz?
As if a Wizard brings good news
or gives the Queen sufficient cause.

Off with your head, you wicked thing!
Oh, girl who sips her beautiful soup,
now paint the roses red and sing
"où est ma chatte," the Dormouse snoop

just might be snoozing during tea—
the Emerald City awaits you there,
with soldiers dressed, and whiskers green
find Glinda with her golden hair.

Oh, girl who sips her beautiful soup—
White Rabbit reads and strokes his fur;
she clicks her heels three times for guilt—
they told me you had been to her.

Cricket Love

Since you were born a katydid, a chirp
your calling song, acoustic winged-sails
with veins of teeth to serenade along
each evening made for crooning cricket tales.
And if your body shade turns green, then hope
will find me soon, unless you live inside
a cage predicting wealth or rain at noon—
lest weather your forte, so please confide
in me before the wedding bells might ring.
A katydid a katy-don't depends
on woo-ability. One thing I'd like
to know up front, it's rumored through some friends
your love is for Pinocchio, please tell
me that's not so, dear Jiminy—oh well.

She Walks in Cruelty

She walks in cruelty like the night
with starless dreams and vacant eyes,
and all that's dimmed by pause of light
hides deep within a thousand lies
forgotten when our lips press tight
as rapture lives inside her thighs.

If one was left alone to guess
or muse unscathed a heartless face
her air would dupe, I dare confess
how matters hurried pushed the pace—
when two together, both undress
though only one feels love's embrace,

and on the day, long passed the now
when sweet so sweet yet subsequent,
the need for her, no matter how
is gone for good and nothing lent
for hope of more with none to show.
No heart as this is heaven-sent!

Will Work for Ants

No matter that the wingo-what
is larger than the wingo-wheat
it's harder to make jumble-jat
or something close to what they'll eat,

and mucho-more the puddle-pumps
are breeding grounds for lolli-doors
yet pompous-pomps those wingo-whats
get fussy-faced refusing chores.

But still, I've tried to make things clear
to tell them nicely, clean their rooms
which causes every mega-mouse
to scurry from the sound of brooms.

The tebbor-toppers help sometimes,
and wingo-whats like wingo-wheats
prefer to leave the work to me,
and so I'm greedy when I eats.

Perchance a diet made from ants
could lure them if I added salt—
the tebbor-toppers seem quite pleased.
I'll tell the ants it's not my fault.

What's Under Your Kilt

The dress of men in skirts these days seems wrong—
and certainly unnerving when a breeze
from somewhere over yonder comes along,
a blast of air that rustles past the trees.
One tricky gust of wind without a sound
that somehow blew a shamrock in my eye,
unfortunately, lifted from the ground.
Who said a three-leaf clover couldn't fly?
And though I'd lost my vision on that day,
those Irish men stood proud in kilts of gold
in all their glory, hand-stitched pleat array—
they made excuses saying it was cold
as if I'd seen a private part or two
that shrunk to dwarfish size when no one knew.

Six Impossible Things after Reading Alice

Let's solve the things I can't erase,
small mysteries that find a place

inside my mind, and out again,
I'd like to take a tour of Heaven.

Round-trip, returning back to earth
through whitish clouds and planned rebirth,

my mother wearing Christmas shoes
while sipping eggnog mixed with booze—

our daily lives divinely blessed,
with burdens gone from those oppressed.

Each suicide at last explained,
the world's problems all contained.

I'd like to know why lives collide—
name Love our home, none left denied.

About the Author

Carol Lynn Stevenson Grellas is a ten-time Pushcart Prize nominee and a seven-time Best of the Net nominee. In 2012 she won the Red Ochre Chapbook Contest, with her manuscript, *Before I Go to Sleep.* In 2018 her book *In the Making of Goodbyes* was nominated for a national book award, and her poem "A Mall in California" received 2nd place for the Jack Kerouac Poetry Prize. In 2019 her chapbook *An Ode to Hope in the Midst of Pandemonium* was a finalist in the Eric Hoffer Book Award, and two sonnets, "James Joyce and Nora Have a Heart-to-Heart in Heaven" and "Eight in the Morning" received Honorable Mentions in the Soul-Making Keats Literary Competition. Her poems have appeared in hundreds of journals online and in print, including, *Verse Daily* and *The Yale Journal of Humanities in Medicine.* She was recently the guest speaker at the California Writer's Club, Sacramento chapter. She is the Editor-in-Chief for *The Orchards Poetry Journal* and Co-Editor-in-Chief for the *Tule Review.* Carol Lynn is a member of the Sacramento Poetry Center Board of Directors, Saratoga Author's Hall of Fame, and is currently enrolled in the Vermont College of Fine Arts MFA in Writing program.

www.ingramcontent.com/pod-product-compliance
Lightning Source LLC
Chambersburg PA
CBHW020214090426
42734CB00008B/1070